You're Aboard Spaceship Earth

by Patricia Lauber
illustrated by Holly Keller

HarperCollins*Publishers*

The illustrations in this book were done with watercolor and black pen on Rives BFK paper.

The *Let's-Read-and-Find-Out Science* book series was originated by Dr. Franklyn M. Branley, Astronomer Emeritus and former Chairman of the American Museum–Hayden Planetarium, and was formerly co-edited by him and Dr. Roma Gans, Professor Emeritus of Childhood Education, Teachers College, Columbia University. Text and illustrations for each of the books in the series are checked for accuracy by an expert in the relevant field. For more information on Let's-Read-and-Find-Out Science books, write to HarperCollins Children's Books, 10 East 53rd Street, New York, NY 10022.

HarperCollins®, ☙®, and Let's Read-and-Find-Out Science® are
trademarks of HarperCollins Publishers Inc.

YOU'RE ABOARD SPACESHIP EARTH

Library of Congress Cataloging-in-Publication Data
Lauber, Patricia
    You're aboard spaceship Earth / by Patricia Lauber ; illustrated by Holly Keller
        p.   cm. — (Let's-read-and-find-out science. Stage 2)
    ISBN 0-06-024407-0. — ISBN 0-06-024408-9 (lib. bdg.)
    ISBN 0-06-445159-3 (pbk.)
    1. Earth—Juvenile literature.   I. Keller, Holly, ill.   II. Title.   III. Series.
QB631.4.L39   1996   94-18704
550—dc20   CIP
                                                                                  AC

Typography by Elynn Cohen
10 9 8 7 6 5 4 3 2 1
❖
First Edition

You're Aboard
Spaceship Earth

The shuttle is blasting off into space.

The shuttle carries a crew of six. For a week the shuttle will be their home in space. On board they have all the things they need to stay alive and healthy.

They have food. They have water. And they have oxygen. Oxygen is the gas that our bodies take from air when we breathe.

Once they are in space, the crew cannot stop somewhere for a snack and a cold drink. They cannot open the windows for some fresh air. They cannot get more of anything. Whatever they need must be on board.

Someday you may rocket into space.
But right now you are aboard a different
spaceship. You have been aboard it all
your life. This spaceship's name is Earth.
   Earth is your home in space. It is home
for every person in the world. We are all
aboard the same spaceship.

67,000 MILES PER HOUR

Earth is one of nine planets that travel around the sun. Every day Earth travels 1,608,000 miles through space. It whizzes along at 67,000 miles an hour. Because we are aboard Earth, we too are whizzing through space.

Like the shuttle crew, we can't make stops. We can't get more of anything. But Spaceship Earth has everything we need to stay alive. It has food. It has air with oxygen. It has water.

Earth has had the same water for billions of years. Plants, animals, and people all use it. Yet Earth doesn't run out of water, because the same water is used over and over again—it is recycled.

Most of our water comes from the oceans. Water is drawn into the air by the sun's heat. It becomes a gas called water vapor. Salt from the ocean water is left behind.

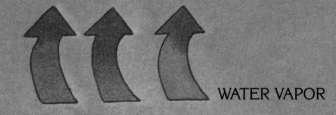

WATER VAPOR

RAIN

Water vapor forms clouds. Rain clouds drop their water on
the earth. Some of it falls in the oceans. Some falls on land.
There much of the rainwater runs off into streams. The
streams flow into rivers. And the rivers flow back into
the oceans.

Again the sun's heat draws water out of the oceans.
Water vapor forms clouds. It falls again as rain.

Water is used in many ways.

The roots of plants draw water from the soil.

Animals drink water and bathe in it.

So do people.

Rushing water can be put to work. It can turn machines that make electricity.

Paper mills use water. Other factories do too.

Tugs and barges travel on rivers. So do canoes and rowboats.

Water fills swimming pools. Heated, it warms buildings in cold weather. It washes clothes, dishes, and cars.

How many other uses can you think of?

But after being used, water goes back into the oceans, is drawn into the air, and falls again as rain. Some of the rain that falls on you probably fell on the dinosaurs.

The air is made of several gases. One of them is oxygen. People and animals all need oxygen.

When you breathe in, your lungs take oxygen out of the air. The oxygen passes into your blood and is used by your body.

When you breathe out, your lungs get rid of a waste gas that your body has made. This gas is called carbon dioxide.

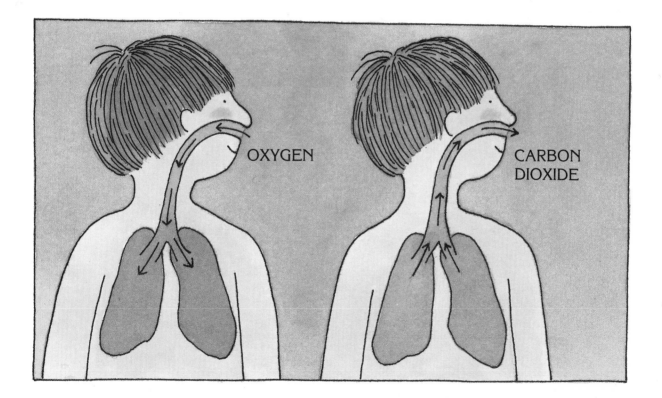

OXYGEN

CARBON DIOXIDE

Animals and people have been using oxygen for a very long time. Yet the oxygen is not all used up. The reason is that green plants keep putting oxygen into the air as they make their food.

Some green plants live in the oceans. Some live on land. All make their food in the same way. They take in water and minerals. They take in carbon dioxide. Using sunlight as energy, they put these things together and make their own food.

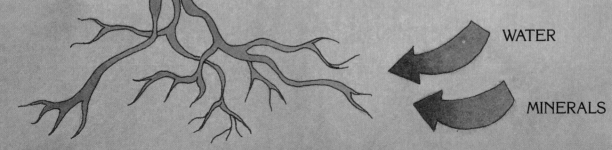

CARBON DIOXIDE

WATER

MINERALS

As they make food, green plants also make oxygen. For them, oxygen is a waste gas. They get rid of oxygen by putting it into the air.

People and animals use the oxygen and put carbon dioxide into the air. Green plants use carbon dioxide and put oxygen into the air. And that is why Spaceship Earth does not run out of oxygen.

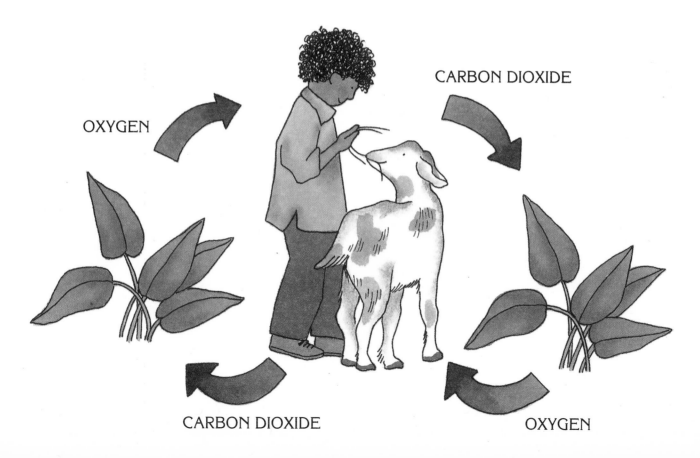

OXYGEN

CARBON DIOXIDE

CARBON DIOXIDE

OXYGEN

Besides making oxygen, Earth's forests and grasslands offer food and shelter to Earth's animals. To grow and be healthy, all these green plants need minerals, which they take from the soil. In nature the minerals are never used up. They too are recycled.

Some of the minerals stay in plants. Some become part of animals—of animals that eat plants, and of animals that eat the plant-eaters. Animals need minerals for growth and health, just as plants do.

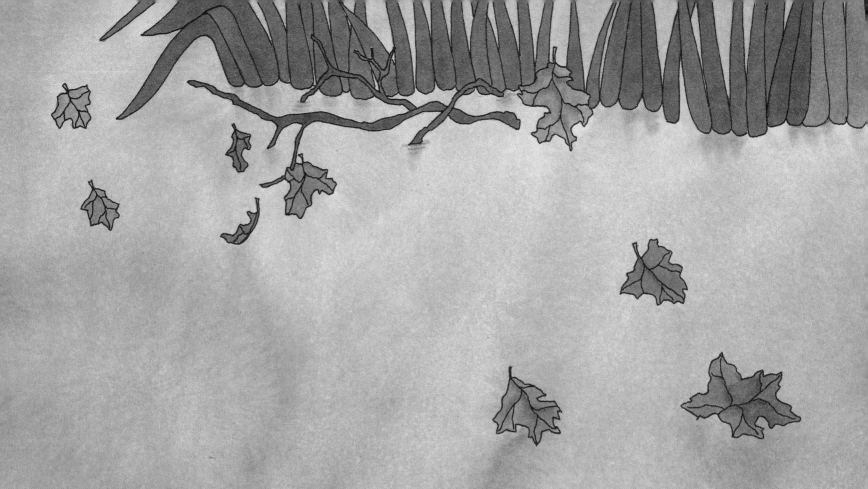

But the minerals do not stay in plants and animals forever. Sooner or later they go back to the soil.

Trees shed their leaves. Branches snap off. Animals leave their waste droppings. Petals, fruits, and seeds fall to the ground. Plants die, and so do animals.

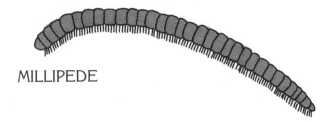

MILLIPEDE

MITES

All this dead matter is rich in minerals. In time, green plants will be able to use them. But first the dead matter must be changed. It is changed by many small forms of life, which feed on it, cause it to rot, and break it down into smaller pieces. Earthworms, millipedes, beetles, mites, and bacteria all help with this work.

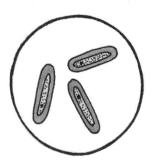

BACTERIA

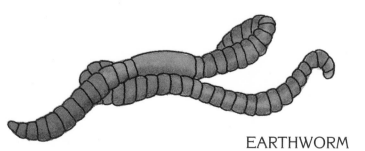

BEETLE

EARTHWORM

Earthworms, for example, may feed on fallen leaves.
Earthworm droppings form a kind of soil. This soil is rich in
minerals released from the dead leaves. Now the minerals can
be used again by green plants. They have been recycled.

Today much of our food comes from farms. When crops are sent to market, minerals go with them and leave the farm. To keep raising healthy crops, farmers must put minerals back in the soil. That is why they fertilize their fields.

Many home gardeners like to recycle minerals, to do what nature does. They put grass clippings, carrot tops, potato peelings, and other plant parts in compost piles. There the dead matter is changed by small forms of life. It becomes rich soil for gardens, with ready-to-use minerals.

See Nature Recycle Minerals

Look for a place where leaves fall off trees and nobody rakes them away. Here leaves pile up year after year. Every autumn a new layer is added.

Take a good look at the top layer of leaves. Do you see any signs that small creatures have been eating them?

Gently lift part of the top layer. How do the older leaves look? What parts of them have been eaten? Do you see any small creatures rushing away from the light?

Using a small spade or a forked branch, go down as many layers as you can. Notice what has happened to the leaves.

What do you find at the bottom? Do you see earthworms? Are there beetles or other small animals? Where have all the old leaves gone, the ones that piled up years ago? Have you come to what looks like rich soil? If so, you have seen how nature breaks down leaves. You have seen how minerals from dead matter go back into the soil to be used again.

Food, water, oxygen—Earth has them all. It's a great spaceship to be aboard! Our job is to keep it that way.

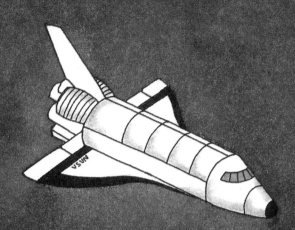

All of us need to understand how Earth works. We need to keep it clean and green. We need to remember that Earth is our home in space, that it is really Spaceship Earth.